Analyzing Notes in the Book of Matthew: Fulfillments of Old Testament Prophecies

Notes in the New Testament, Volume 1

Bible Sermons

Published by Seminit Publications, 2023.

While every precaution has been taken in the preparation of this book, the publisher assumes no responsibility for errors or omissions, or for damages resulting from the use of the information contained herein.

ANALYZING NOTES IN THE BOOK OF MATTHEW: FULFILLMENTS OF OLD TESTAMENT PROPHECIES

First edition. February 26, 2023.

Copyright © 2023 Bible Sermons.

ISBN: 979-8215847794

Written by Bible Sermons.

Table of Contents

Matthew 2:9. *when they had heard the king, they departed; And, LO, the star, which they saw in the east, went before them, until it came and stood where the child was.*

Probably it was not a star in the sense in which we use the word: that is a planet, or a fixed star; But a meteoric brightness, which moved in the sky, and also guided the wise men. They do not seem to have seen its light after they turn aside on their journey; it led them to the region of Judea, so they came to the capital city, Jerusalem. When they left Herod, the star appeared again, and led them to the little town of Bethlehem, where they found Christ. God can sometimes send us stars, bright lights of joy, to guide us on our way; He can also bring them back, and then we must walk by faith. When they reappear, we will be glad to have them once more, for wise men they were.

— **Charles Spurgeon**

Introduction

Before his conversion, Matthew the son of Alphaeus collected taxes in Capernaum on behalf of the Romans. At that time his name was Levi, Mark 2:14. The Lord commanded him to follow him, and he did. It is probable that he changed his name after this; Matthew means "gift of God". He had been a servant of the greatest earthly kingdom known up to that time, the Roman Empire. It is fitting, then, that his Gospel has much to tell us of a much greater empire, the kingdom of God.

The first Gospel records a high percentage of Jesus' teachings. More than half consists of his parables and sayings. The people continually marveled at his teaching; 7:28, 13:54, 22:33. Apart from its introduction and conclusion, the Gospel can be divided into five sections, each of which ends with words such as, "when Jesus had finished all these words," See 7.28, 11.1, 13.53, 19.1, 26.1.

It is almost certain that Matthew wrote his Gospel for the Jews. To them, the humiliation, rejection and death of Jesus was a real stumbling block. They had been waiting for one who would deliver them militarily and politically, Luke 24:21. Matthew set out to show that Jesus was truly their Messiah. Chapter 1 shows that His genealogy was accurate; He was entitled to the promises of Abraham and the throne of David. Chapter 2 shows that His childhood was in complete agreement with the Old Testament.

Chapter 3 shows that the prophesied forerunner had already come. Chapter 4 shows that His temptation proved that He was capable of reigning. Chapters 5 through 7 detail the principles under which He would rule. Chapters 8 and 9 record the fulfillment of the messianic signs of Isaiah 35 and 61. All the important events of Jesus' life took place to fulfill the Old Testament prophecies. Ten times Matthew uses words like "that the prophets might be fulfilled".

Note the expression, "From that time Jesus began" in 4:17 and 16:21. Broadly speaking, then, the Gospel consists of three parts: an introduction from 1:1 to 4:16; the ministry of Jesus from 4:17 to 16:20; and, his path of suffering and glory, from 16:21 to 28:20.

Chapter 1
The Birth of Jesus Christ

Three times reference is made to Mary giving birth to a son, 1:21, 23, 25. A woman had played a role in making man a sinner, Genesis 3; a woman played a role in bringing him a Savior. The child, 2.11, was Mary's son, 1.25, the fruit of her womb, Luke 1.25. But twice it is emphasized that this child was of the Holy Spirit, 1.18, 20, which he had to be, because he was God, 1.23. We do not understand how legitimate and holy humanity was united in one person with the eternal Godhead, 11.27, 1 Timothy 3.16. But we gladly believe that which we do not explain, for God has revealed it "to us and to our children forever," Deuteronomy 29.29.

In becoming flesh, John 1.14, the eternal Word continued to be what he had always been, but at the same time became what he never was. Melchizedek, a type of Christ, was "without father, without mother," Heb. 7.3. The Lord Jesus was made man and as such had no father, 1.18; he was God and as such had no mother.

The holiness of the child was assured by the Holy Spirit. Jesus came in the flesh,

1 John 4.2, but was sent only in the likeness of sinful flesh, Romans 8.3. He partook of our human nature but not of our sinful nature. Mary was imperfect and needed a Savior, Luke 1.47, but the Holy Spirit could "bring a clean thing out of an unclean thing", Job 14.4 (in the Modern Version, etc.).

"A good name is of more value than great riches," Proverbs 22.1. The Lord would be known by two good names, 1.21, 23, and Luke tells us of a third.

He would be called the Son of God, Luke 1:35,

For what it had always been.

He would be called Immanuel, 1.23, for what he became.

He would be called Jesus, 1.21, because of what He was going to do.

Isaac, "laughter," was named before his birth because of something his father had done, Gen. 17:17 to 19, but Jesus received his name before he was born because of something he himself was going to do. He was going to save, 1.21.

"The days of his flesh," Hebrews 5.7, began with the huge step from the high throne of God down into the womb of a woman, and would end with yet another step down into the unfathomable depths of the suffering of the cross, Matthew 26.38,39, 27.46.

Chapter 2
Born King

The little child Jesus is the center of interest in the whole chapter. Every time mention is made of the child and his mother together, He is given first place, 2.11, 13, 20,21. Once Jesus is presented as the leader in 2.6, Herod is not mentioned again as the king; compare 2.13 with 2.7, 12,13, 15, 16, 19,22. The rightful "king of the Jews" had arrived!

The little child was at the same time the object of Satan's interest. Revelation pulls the curtain aside and shows that the devil was the real instigator of Herod's attempt to kill the child. The "dragon" was in expectation of devouring the child "as soon as he was born", Revelation 12:4. From the beginning Satan has been dedicated to thwarting God's purposes in Christ. God originally revealed that the Deliverer to come would be of the seed of the woman, and therefore the devil set out to corrupt and destroy her seed. Satan used Eve's firstborn to kill her second son, but God responded with Seth, Genesis 3.15, 4.1 to 8.25. Then the devil was the mastermind behind an attack against "the daughters of men," in order to corrupt their seed, Genesis 6.1, 2, Jude 6, but God responded with the flood.

God later revealed that the Deliverer would be from the seed of Abraham. The serpent tried to corrupt it by the machinations of the flesh, Genesis 16, but God responded with Isaac. The Pharaohs were the next unnoticed tools to attack the seed of Abraham, but God responded with Moses, Exodus 1 to 14. God had also implied that the Deliverer would be from the tribe of Judah, Genesis 49:10, and later, when one from that royal tribe was highlighted, the devil used the envious Saul to make several attempts on young David's life, "but God did not give him into his hand," 1 Samuel 23:14.

Then it was made known that the Deliverer would be of the seed of David,

From among his many sons, David chose Solomon, 1 Kings 1.17. Satan attacked through Adonijah but to no effect, 1 Kings 1. The devil made another attempt against David's seed 150 years later through Athaliah, but God presented the infant Joash, 2 Kings 11.Like so many before him, Herod played the role of the serpent's seed, but Mary's son was irrevocably destined for God's throne, Rev. 12.5.

Chapter 3
The Baptism of Christ

John's message was as simple as his clothing and diet, 3.2, 4. He took as his commands the words of Isaiah the prophet, and thus fearlessly announced the requirement to repent, Matthew 3.3, Isaiah 40.3, John 1.23,

Three different classes were presented for baptism. There was the vast multitude of 3.5, 6. Great numbers of people flocked from the city of Jerusalem, the province of Judea, and the banks of the Jordan. Among the crowd were publicans and harlots who believed the preaching of John the Baptist, 21:32. They came with genuine repentance, and confession of their sins accompanied their baptism.

There was a considerable group in 3:7-12, composed of Pharisees and Sadducees. Among them were many hypocrites who took refuge in their national privileges and saw no need for personal repentance. John had some stern things to say to them without reservation.

There was the lone person, 3:13 to 17. "Then Jesus came". Unlike the crowd, He manifested no signs of repentance. He confessed nothing because there were no actions for Him to regret, no words of His to retract, no thoughts for which to be ashamed. Little wonder, then, that John doubted that he should baptize him. Nevertheless, it was fitting that Christ should identify himself with his people, 3.15.

The Spirit descended and came upon Him. As the offering baked in a frying pan was kneaded with oil, Leviticus 2:5, so the beginning and character of Christ's human nature depended on the Holy Spirit, 1:18, 20, of whom the oil is recognized as a symbol. As the oil was then poured upon the offering, Leviticus 2.6, so the Lord was anointed on this occasion with the Holy Spirit, Acts 10.38.

With words that echoed messianic prophecies - Psalm 27 and Isaiah 42:1 - God testified that He was pleased with His beloved Son. The same words would be heard again on the Mount of Transfiguration, 17:5. On the second occasion, the Father would declare His satisfaction with the Savior's public ministry; at the Jordan, He declared His entire pleasure with the years of privacy in Nazareth.

Blessed is our Savior: in public and in private, always perfect!

4.1 to 18

The Temptation of the Messiah

The devil's purpose was to dissuade Jesus from His messianic mission as it had been established for Him by God's will. The popular image of the coming Messiah was one of a military deliverer who would bring Israel to safety and establish a great earthly empire with Israel as its center. God's program for the Messiah also ended in a throne, but by passing through a cross, Luke 24:26. The wilderness temptations would make clear what kind of Messiah Jesus was.

Satan first attempted to drive in the point of his wedge. Without making any reference to Christ's mission, he launched his attack with the apparently unrelated subject of food, 4.3. It was not admissible, Satan implied, that the King of Israel should starve in the wilderness; surely he could avail himself of his Messianic powers to meet his modest needs! The question, however, extended far beyond stones and bread. If the devil could persuade Jesus to act independently of God's will in a small matter, it was likely that he would later succeed in doing so in larger matters, such as the cross.

The relevance of the second temptation was more obvious. If Jesus, in response to Satan's skillful use of Psalm 91:11, 12, had thrown himself from the pinnacle of the temple, the crowd of parishioners in the courtyard below would have served as sure witnesses. Seeing his descent amidst angelic escort, they would recognize the Lord who would have come "suddenly to his temple", Malachi 3.1. He could have gained immediate followers if only he had conformed to the popular concept of the Messiah, offering some shocking spectacle.

Finally the devil cast aside all disguise and manifested himself openly. He blatantly offered Jesus all the kingdoms of the earth in exchange for his homage. To compromise with Him, Satan reasoned, was a small price to pay to get Golgotha out of the way. The Son of Man could enter His glory without suffering! But Jesus' future path had already been chosen. The path laid down by God was more costly, but it was the one He was going to take.

Jesus defeated the devil with three quotes from the last of the five books of Moses. Like David, he carried five "stones" but needed only one, 1 Samuel 17:40, 49.

4.11 to 25

Leaving

———

The passage relates four instances of leaving something. Satan left the Lord, 4:11; Jesus left Nazareth, 4:13; Peter and Andrew left their nets, 4:20; James and John left their boat, 4:22.

Satan left the Lord because he had been defeated. He had run out of ammunition. He had performed every form of temptation, Luke 4 13, but none of his fiery darts had succeeded in discovering combustible material in the Lord Jesus! In the Jordan Jesus had fulfilled all righteousness, 3.15, and in the wilderness He had resisted every temptation. Having bound the strong man, Jesus proceeded to plunder his goods, 12.29, for his ministry of healing and casting out demons.

Possibly Jesus' withdrawal followed the events narrated in Luke 4:16-30. As it was, he left Nazareth because he had been rejected, 4:13. Because of their unbelief, the men of Nazareth lost both his presence and his blessings. Capernaum, not Nazareth, would thus be the scene of most of her mighty works; she would be "lifted up to heaven," 11.23, both in privileges and in her self-pride.

Capernaum means "village of Nahum," and a tradition in Galilee states that it was the burial place of the prophet Nahum. It was fitting, indeed, that the streets of Capernaum were walked by One who brought the good news and announced the peace that Nahum had expressed in 1.15 of his prophecy almost 700 years earlier. Now Zebulun could avail himself of "the hidden treasures" and Naphtali was indeed "full of the blessing of the Lord," Deuteronomy 33.19, 23.

The four fishermen left the boat because they had been recruited. He required them to leave their trade and constantly accompany him as his pupils and disciples. Peter and Andrew were called to a higher fishing, just as David was once called to a higher form of shepherding, Psalm 78:70-72. They were not like the Chaldean "fishermen" who fished the land of Judah to take the people captive, Jeremiah 16:16. Rather, they were to be fishermen of salvation. It is exciting to recognize that the Lord called humble fishermen instead of angels, 4:11, to be his evangelists,

2 Corinthians 4.7.

5.1 to 16
True Beatitude

The content of chapters 5 to 7 is often called the Sermon on the Mount. It is the magna carta of the kingdom of heaven. Jesus began his message in the same way that the book of Psalms begins, namely, with a description of the truly blessed man.

The measurement of blessedness is very different from that of the world. The world congratulates and counts as happy those who achieve riches, fame or easy life. Happiness for the unconverted is usually found in honors, material goods or sensual pleasure. Christ measures blessedness in a very different way. His description of the ideal citizen of his kingdom ran counter to ideas about what was involved in belonging to that kingdom.

The Jews generally expected the beatitude of the kingdom to consist of authority, comfort, and plenty. The Lord's manifesto dealt a rude blow to this expectation, 5.3 to 12. The citizens of the kingdom would have humble views of themselves; they would mourn over sin; they would be meek and peaceable; they would be eager to please God; they would show sympathy and generosity to others in need; they would be concerned with inward purity (rather than outward cleanliness, like the Pharisees) and would be peace-loving, seeking peace. Far from gaining them respect, these characteristics would attract opposition.

Jesus had lived his sermon for thirty years before preaching it. To some extent these beatitudes constitute his self-portrait. He was humble of heart, 11:29. He lamented the effect of sin on others, 23.37, 38. He was meek, 11.29, 21.5. His food was the doing of his Father's will, John 4.34.

He manifested mercy and compassion, Matthew 9.27 to 30. He was, and is, pure, 1 John 3.3 to 5. He has made peace, Colossians 1.20. He was cruelly persecuted and cursed, 1 Peter 2.23. Therefore, the description of the ideal citizen of the kingdom was that of its King.

The disciples who put these beatitudes into practice are salt and light in the midst of a corrupt world that is surrounded by spiritual darkness, 5:13-16. Whoever turns away from the surrounding reality to seclude himself in the style of the monk is forgetting the lesson of the light.

5.17 to 48

Law Enforcement

———

The Lord had not come in order to displace the law, but to fulfill it. That is to say, He would explain its full meaning and what it implied, penetrating beneath His words to the spirit of the law and the principles that supported it. His dispute was not with the law itself but with the scribes and Pharisees. It behooves us to meditate on three rules-indeed, three "if not"-that the Lord laid down for entrance into his kingdom: repentance, 18.3; new birth, John 3.5; right conduct, 5.20.

5.20 sets out the whole theme of the sermon. The scribes were teachers of theology and had received years of preparation. The Pharisees were groups of pious laymen from all sectors of society; only their leaders were theologians. Jesus spoke of three types of piety: that of the theologians, that of the religious laity, and that of his disciples. He dealt first with the false interpretation of spiritual righteousness, given by the theologians, 5:21 to 48. He continued his controversy with the righteousness of the Pharisees; almsgiving, prayers and fasting were the outstanding characteristics of their piety, 6:1 to 18.

In 5:21-48 the Lord gave a spiritual exposition of the law. His authority to do this is emphatically emphasized six times, "But I say unto you." He revealed something of the great demands of the law, even when legalism had limited it to mere outward conformity. He spoke also of the disciple's attitude to his brother, 5:21 to 26; to women, 5:27 to 30; to marriage, 5:31, 32; truthful conversation, 5:33 to 37; violence, 5:38 to 42; and to his enemy, 5:43 to 48.

He warned his followers not to hate one another, 5.22, 1 John 3.15, and gave them advice on how to behave if others gave them cause to hate them. Note the first concerning reconciliation of an offended brother, 5.24; interest in the kingdom of God, 6.33; and self-judgment, 7.5. Jesus required unrelenting severity for anything that proved to be a temptation to carnality, 5.28 to 30. Secret oaths, which had turned out to be a subterfuge to deceive, were forbidden. One was not to resist in case of being treated unjustly; the disciple would win by losing! There was nothing praiseworthy in simply loving one's own, 5.45-47.

6.1 to 18

Prayer

———

The Lord spoke concerning almsgiving, vv 1 to 4; prayer, vv 5 to 15; and fasting, vv 16 to 18. The first is an action directed to one's fellow man, the second to God, and the third to oneself. Christ condemned the man who gave alms with the sound of a trumpet, the man who placed himself in places of greater visibility to pray, and the man who disfigured his face to make it known that he was fasting.

The first character desired to be praised by men; the second to be seen of men; and the third to show men that he fasted. Of each, the Lord said that he had already had his reward. His words meant that such had already acknowledged receipt of their payment. There was no balance left to carry forward for heavenly approval! Religious gestures one makes to gain applause are worthless in the Father's esteem.

Regarding prayer, the Lord had something to say about the place, the manner, and the content. That is, he gave instructions about where, how, and what to pray. Jesus had no room for pantomime, nor for hollow prayer or vain repetition, vv 5 to 8. The prayer from 9 to 13 is impressive for its brevity, simplicity and scope. It contains only seventy-one words and can be repeated in thirty seconds. Yet it is a true compendium of prayer, with petitions ranging from the common necessity of breakfast to the eternal purposes of God. It puts God's glory first and our needs second. While routine matters are not too insignificant to be mentioned, the prayer recognizes the supremacy of the spiritual.

Prayer begins with an intimate, filial approach, but at the same time maintains due holy reverence. The disciple in prayer then asks for God's absolute command among men, when earth will reciprocate with a righteous reflection of His will even as heaven does at present. Leaving the cosmic plan of the ages, he concentrates on present needs, daily and physical. Finally, he asks forgiveness for any past faults and to be delivered from those that may arise. Taking full account of his own weakness and the devil's deceit and skill, the disciple exhibits a sense of complete self-distrust.

6.19 to 34
Heaven or Earth

———

The previous section raises the question of whether in religious activities we seek approval from God or from men, whether from heaven or from earth; 6.1 to 18. The choice between heaven and earth occupies the rest of the chapter as well. Riches can be accumulated for the one or the other; 6.19 to 21. Treasure in heaven represents the best investment and offers the greatest security. The world says of its wealth that one cannot carry it with him. True, 1 Timothy 6.7, but the Lord says we can send it ahead!

The disciple should have as a dominant purpose in his life that of seeking the "kingdom of God", 6.33. His eyes should be fixed on heavenly approval and its treasure. Selfishness, like a film, obscures the vision and prevents the true light from entering the soul. The believer must choose who or what will govern his life. He cannot serve God and money. Since the disciple cannot fix his affections on heavenly and earthly values at the same time (note how 6.25 begins with therefore), he must devote all energy to the former and renounce all longing for the latter. He knows that God will provide for all his needs, 6.25 to 34.

Worries about the daily chores can be as harmful spiritually as the love of money, 13.22. Anxiety is not only sterile, but unnecessary. We should not be anxious about what we put before or on our bodies. God gave both life and body, and will also provide lesser things such as food and clothing. We are worth "much more" than the birds, and the Father will do for us "much more" than He will do for the flowers.

The things of this world are of value to the unbeliever; he seeks "all these things". The believer seeks first the kingdom of God. For him, it is the spiritual things that have the greatest value, and the rest is of little importance. God takes care of his earthly needs. The worldly man actively pursues the "things" of this world; the disciple receives them from his Father. He is interested in God's interests and God is interested in his. We should be free from earthly anxiety because He knows what we need, 6.32; because He hears our prayers, Philippians 4.6; and because He cares for us, 1 Peter 5.7. With such a three-fold cord, Ecclesiastes 4.12, we can face "tomorrow" without fear or anxiety, 6.34.

Chapter 7
Hearing and Doing

The Lord's comments on the judgment of others do not refer to civil courts as in Romans 13, nor to church discipline, 1 Corinthians 5. They refer to the private and despicable judgment of others, which arises from antipathy, a partisan spirit and envy. This unnecessary criticism finds no place in the life of a disciple who humbly acknowledges his own faults. As one grows in grace, he becomes more severe in his judgment of himself and more tolerant in his judgment of others.

Confident and persistent prayer is the disciple's resource in every need. God gives "good things to those who ask him", 7.11, James 1.17. We often err in requests and ask incorrectly in the desire to achieve something right; in effect, we ask for a snake! God, however, takes our faulty vision into account, and in His loving wisdom provides something better, Ephesians 3.20. He never leaves us worse off or mocks us.

The Lord closes his sermon with a call to discipleship, speaking of two roads, two trees and two foundations. No effort is required to walk the broad way. One enters it through a door that accommodates worldly ambitions, lust and greed. Instead, it requires purpose and steadfastness to enter and proceed along the narrow path that leads to the only life of worth.

The man on the broad way says that life consists in accumulating, abusing, avenging. The man on the narrow way accepts Christ's teaching that life is about giving, humbling oneself and turning the cheek. The first series is "bad fruits" and the second "good fruits". The fruits determine the nature of the tree. A great profession and showy exploits do not assure entrance into the kingdom of God; it is achieved only by submission to the will of the Father.

This will is made known in "words" of the Lord, 7.24 to 27. The foolish man lives by the world's standards. The wise man practices the sayings of Christ and conforms to the golden rule in 7.12, where the Lord sums up the whole law and the prophets in one simple statement; "he who loves his neighbor has fulfilled the law," Romans 13.8. It is love put into action. Jesus does not demand that we barely listen to him and understand his sayings, let alone simply applaud them. Ezekiel 33:31, 32 speaks of those who "hear thy words, and do them not; but with their mouth they flatter with their lips, and their heart followeth after their covetousness. And, behold, thou art unto them as a singer of sweetness, fair of voice, and singing well: and they will hear thy words, but will not do them." But the Lord demands that we put his sayings into practice!

Chapter 8
His Word and Hand

Several events are narrated here that illustrate the truth that "the word of the king is with power," Ecclesiastes 8.4. The authority of the King's word prevailed over the ravages of sickness in 8.5 to 13. A servant was paralyzed and severely tormented, but his master had faith in Christ without limit. "Only say the word," he pleaded. Great was the centurion's compassion and great his humility, 8.5 to 8 with Luke 7.4, and great his faith too. The Lord marveled at so much faith, somewhat as his disciples were to marvel at so much power in verse 27. The centurion's faith exceeded that of the leper, 8.2, and left far behind that of the disciples, 8.25, 26.

The word of the Lord had power also over Satan's representatives. "By the word he cast out demons." In verses 28 to 34 an example is given of his dominion over Satan's forces and kingdom. The demons could present their request, but ultimately they depended on his command. One word from the King was enough: "Go," and they were gone.

Finally, His word controlled the violence of the sea. In the storm He slept "on a headboard", Mark 4.38. We note that a little earlier He had said that He had nowhere to lay His head, 8.20. Possibly some consecrated ear had listened, some devoted heart had been touched, and some tender hand had provided where He might rest. He arose and muzzled the tempest. It was a case of Psalm 148.8: "The storm wind that performeth his word."

His word had power; He needed no more. Therefore, it is pleasing to note the two occasions when He stretched out His hand: 8.3, 15. How tender His touch, and how grateful He was! As far as we know, Jesus had not healed a leper before this occasion, and it is apparent that the man in 8.2 was unsure that he would do so. Nevertheless, he trusted in Jesus' power. The leper here said, "you can," in contrast to the man in Mark 9.22 who said, "if you can do anything." Today the Lord says "I will" to those who suffer from the leprosy of sin. They enjoy the cleansing, 8.3, His presence, Hebrews 13.5, and the hope of His return, John 14.3.

Chapter 9
The Physician

We are struck by the effects that the Lord's miracles had on those who saw and heard him, 9.8, 26, 31, 33. Great must have been the rejoicing of those who experienced their power in themselves. Had they chosen to express their joy in the form of a song ("Is anyone joyful? Sing praises," James 5.13), they would have found no better words than those of Psalm 103.3 to 5, where David gave five descriptions of the Lord ("He it is who forgives all your iniquities, who heals all your diseases; who rescues your life from the pit, who crowns you with favors and mercies; who satisfies your mouth with good so that you are rejuvenated like an eagle)."

For the paralytic man, it was the God "who forgives all his iniquities",

9:1 to 7. The man owed much to the faith of his friends, who overcame every obstacle and obtained an even greater blessing than he had expected. The bed that had been a symbol of his sickness became a symbol of health and salvation. For the woman with the issue of blood, it was the God "who heals all your diseases," 9:20-22. Such was the overflowing compassion of the Lord that He performed one gracious work while He was on the way to do another.

For Jairus' daughter He was "the one who rescues your life from the pit", 9:18, 19, 23 to 26. His promise was to awaken her, and she arose. For the two men who cried for mercy, it was the God who "crowns with favor and mercy", 9.27 to 31. The eyes of the blind man were opened by the Son of David, who came to save, 20.30, Isaiah 35.4, 5. Finally, for the dumb demoniac, it was the God who "satisfies your mouth with good", 9:32, 33.

In the middle of the section recording these exploits, the Great Physician likens the sinful rejects around him to a sick man, seeing the disease as an apt picture of the effects of sin. We are given several representations of the sinner. He lacks strength to walk aright, 9.2, but the gospel is the power of God, Romans 1.16, 5.6. He is defiled, 9.20, scourged, Mark 5.29, unclean, Leviticus 15.25 to 30, but the gospel cleanses, 1 John 1.7. The sinner is dead in his sins, 9.18, but the gospel gives life, Ephesians 2.1 to 5. He is blinded by the god of this world, 9.27, but the gospel enlightens, 2 Corinthians 4.4 to 6. He cannot say anything to confess his state, 9.32, nor can he praise, but the gospel loosens the tongue-tie, Romans 10.9, 1 Peter 2.5.

Bless the Lord, O my soul! Psalm 103:2.

Chapter 10
All Needs Satisfied

The Lord commissioned his apostles. "Go," he said in 10:6. But before they were sent out, "he gave them authority." The Lord always provides strength again in connection with the task he assigns. From the day David was anointed king, the Spirit of Jehovah came upon him, 1 Samuel 16.13. If Elisha was to be prophet in Elijah's place, 1 Samuel 19.16, then he would receive a double portion of his spirit, 2 Kings 2.9 to 15.

When the Lord calls, he always enables one and supplies one's need. Jesus instructed the disciples to whom they should go, what to do and say, vv 5 to 8, and explained how they would receive their support, vv 9 to 13. He explained how they should act in case the people rejected them and their message. Later he would speak of the eternal rewards that await those who willingly receive his ambassadors, 10:40-42. But before this, in verses 16-39, he takes time to warn his disciples of the severe opposition they would encounter and to give them words of encouragement.

The apostles must have been wise as serpents and harmless as doves, for they would be exposed to death like sheep, unable to protect themselves. They could expect trouble from the authorities, both civil and ecclesiastical, from Jews as well as Gentiles, 10.17, 18, but the Lord assured them that they need not be unduly worried. Even though they were "unlettered" men, Acts 4.13, they could resist their superiors in authority and knowledge, relying on the guidance of the Spirit.

Nor need they be fearful: why fear suffering when it would make them conform to their Master? They could look forward to a time when their integrity and triumph would be openly recognized. They need not be daunted by opponents whose power was limited, for such could harm only the body. Fear has no place in the heart that recognizes that the smallest incidents of life work only for good. God is interested in details; He cares also for the common bird, and how much more for His children. Without anxiety about their words or fear for their safety, disciples must confess Christ and love Him above all others,

10.32 to 39.

Chapter 11
A Restful Soul

The passage emphasizes the occasion and background of Jesus' prayer, vv 25, 26. "At that time," directs us to the somber setting described in the first part of the chapter. John the Baptist had wavered in his faith, confined in the prison of Marcaerus for quite some time now. News of Jesus' works were brought to him, especially the restoration to life of the son of the widow of Nain, Luke 7.18. He did not doubt that Jesus was a great prophet but he was now less certain that he was the Christ. The Messiah was to "publish liberty to the captives,

And to the prisoners opening of the prison", Isaiah 61.1.

John had announced that the kingdom of God was at hand, 3.2. If Jesus was the King, where was the freedom and where was the winnowing and the fire? Jesus invited John to reconsider his works, 11.4 to 6 with Isaiah 35.3 to 6, 61.1, 2. The generation to whom Jesus ministered criticized and mocked his ministry as John's, 11.16 to 19. John was not to their liking because he refused to participate in their pleasures of self-indulgence; he "did not dance," 11.17. They dismissed him as a demon-possessed fanatic. Jesus did not please them either. He refused to stick to the rules of their oral tradition with its hypocritical washing and fasting; "he did not mourn," 11.17. They dismissed him as a glutton. The cities, where Jesus had performed most of his signs, refused to respond with repentance, 11.20 to 24. The most favored area of the land remained in unbelief. All these circumstances combined to discourage. He seemed to have spent His strength "in vain and to no profit," Isaiah 49.4. But He would not grow weary or faint, Isaiah 42.4.

"At that time," Matt. 11.25, he addressed God in praise. When Jacob had folded his hands in blessing Joseph's children, Joseph had exclaimed, "Not so, my father," Genesis 48.17, 18. The Lord saw that in the same way his Father had folded his hands, revealing his secrets to the children but hiding them from the wise. Yet he answered, "Yes, Father, for so it pleased you." In the face of his trials and rejection, the Lord manifested absolute submission to the will and yoke of his Father. In that he found rest for his soul. In the midst of it all, he remained serene and at peace, and today he gives us the same rest.

12.1 to 21
Lawful

The Pharisees were careful to safeguard the interests of their Sabbath. Jesus, however, had already offered men a much greater rest: "I will give you rest" "You will find rest for your souls", 11.28, 29.

The Pharisees criticized the disciples for satisfying their hunger by plucking and eating ears of grain on a Sabbath day; it was not "lawful" to do so. Jesus cited two cases in response: that of David, for whom it was technically not "lawful" to eat the shewbread, Leviticus 24:9 and 1 Samuel 21:6, and, of equal relevance, that of the priesthood in the temple on the Sabbath, Numbers 28:9. In both cases the letter of the Jewish law contradicted major laws and principles. David's action was justified by the priority of the service of God.

The Pharisees had their values completely distorted. Had they grasped the essence of pure religion, they would have pitied the disciples instead of condemning them. The responsibility of the priests in the temple freed them from guilt. How much more then were the disciples free from guilt because of their association with One far greater than the temple! The angel had said of Jesus, "This One will be great," Luke 1:32. In His priestly function, He was greater than the temple, 12.6; in His prophetic function, He was greater than Solomon, 12.42. The Messiah had full authority to direct the style of Sabbath observance and to sanction deeds of necessity on that day, 12.8.

When the Pharisees asked whether it was lawful to heal on the Sabbath, Jesus replied that it was lawful to do good. They saw the healing of the sick as a work that could be avoided; He saw it as an obligation. One does wrong to leave undone a good ministry that is within one's reach. Being, therefore, under an obligation to "do" something, Jesus was doing good! Unlike the popular expectation of a conquering Messiah, the Servant of Jehovah was disdainful of ostentation and self-praise. Even when he was severe with the hypocritical Pharisees, he showed extreme tenderness to the weak and sick, 12:16-20.

12.22 to 50

Power of Satan or of God?

The Pharisees were astonished because the people drew the proper conclusion from the Lord's great healing works, 12:23. Certainly his power could not be explained in merely human terms. Unable to attribute it to the power of God, the Pharisees claimed that Jesus was in league with the devil. The Lord calmly confronted the accusation and broke it to pieces, pointing out the absurd assumption involved in the accusation, namely that Satan was operating against Himself.

No organized society-whether kingdom, city or home-can stand when it is divided. Satan's power was failing, Christ asserted, not because of civil war within but because of an invasion from without. Satan had encountered a force greater than himself. The power of the Spirit of God had intervened; the kingdom of God had suddenly shone upon humanity.

"He who is not against us is for us", Luke 9:50, is the standard of measurement that the disciple employs with regard to others. When examining himself, on the other hand, the test he applies is: "He who is not with me is against me", Matthew 12.30. There is no neutral ground!

Instead of accepting the miracle of Christ as evidence that He was the Messiah, the Pharisees chose to present good as evil and to assign the power of the Spirit to the devil. Such men were determined to reject Jesus and close their eyes to all evidence. For them there was no hope. Nothing more could be done to convince them or lead them to repentance, and without this there would be no forgiveness, 12.31, 32, Mark 3.28 to

30. Jesus emphasized that the tree and its fruit had to be of the same character.

If the casting out of demons (the fruit) was a good work, the power to do it (the tree) had to be good also, 12:33. The Pharisees' accusation revealed the true condition of their hearts. The words were an indication of character and, as such, would be taken as evidence "in the day of judgment." The Lord refused to perform a miracle in order to dazzle the people into accepting Him. Men should have read by faith the Messianic signs already given to them and responded with repentance.

13.1 to 23

Sower, Seed and Soil

———

The seven parables told by Balaam had to do with the nation of Israel, Numbers chapters 23 and 24; the seven parables told by Jesus in Matthew 13 have to do with the kingdom of heaven.

The first of the Lord's parables is that of the Sower. Its importance may be estimated by the fact that it is one of two parables common to all the synoptic gospels. The parable challenges men as to whether they are receiving the "seed," which is "the word of the kingdom," with positive and lasting results. As long as the sower does his task well and the seed is good, the results of the sowing depend on the kind of place where the seed falls.

Jesus describes four types of soil: the side of the road, the stony places, among thorns, and the good soil. In the first case the seed fell on but not in; in the second, it fell in but not down; in the third, it fell down but did not come up again. Only in the fourth case did the seed fall on the earth, enter there, penetrate below, and then grow upward in abundant harvest. It was not eaten, burned or drowned.

The first represents the case where "the word" remains on the surface of one's memory. The mind does not grasp its real meaning, and therefore it is easy for the devil to remove its impact. The second is the case where the person hears the word with enthusiasm but does not really take it to heart. Consequently, the hearer is not prepared to face the trials that come in the form of opposition. The third is the case where someone receives "the word" and gives every appearance and promise of possessing life. But, as the days go by, the effect of that word is blocked and frustrated by the concerns of life itself; by anxiety, material well-being and worldliness, Luke 8.14. The fourth represents the case where "the word" is not only heard and understood but remains and yields results in one's life. The person is "saved;" see Luke 8.12.

A practical point: Jesus said that the sower went out to sow. The sower did not merely publish a notice to say that at such and such a place the gospel would be preached at a certain time, and that therefore the unconverted should come to "be sown." Neither Jesus nor his apostles operated that way!

13.24 to 58

The Kingdom of Heaven

The reading contains six parables. The first three were addressed to the multitude and told outside the house, as was that of the Sower also, 13:1 to 3. The last three were addressed to the disciples, inside the house, 13:36. The first three parables have to do with the appearance and character of what the kingdom of God is on the outside. The last three reveal God's thoughts about the kingdom, and manifest that he has an answer to all the perversity and failure associated with the false profession described in the first three. The one who told the parables possessed great authority, claiming that the world, the angels and the kingdom were his, 13:24, 37-41.

Each of the last three parables corresponds closely to one of the first three. There is a pronounced similarity between the interpretation of the first and the last, 13.40 to 42, 49, 50. The one of the tares teaches that the devil introduces his agents intermingled with "the sons of the kingdom," 13.38, 39. The one of the net teaches that the Lord will separate, in his time and in his way, the good and the bad, 13.48 to 50. The parable of the mustard seed describes how the movement professing the name of Christ will grow from humble beginnings to an impressive worldwide organization, 13:31, 32.

For the symbolism of the tree, the birds and the branches, see Ezekiel 31 and Daniel 4. Possibly the birds of the air represent satanic influence, Luke 8.5, 12. The solitary pearl in verses 45 and 46 is the true church (the body of Ephesians 4.4 to 16) which, while remaining relatively small, is extremely valuable in the eyes of the Lord. In the language of the parable, He "sold all that he had, and bought it". See 2 Corinthians 8:9 and Ephesians 5:25.

One day the pearl will be presented to Him "a glorious church, not having spot or wrinkle or any such thing, but that it should be holy and without blemish," Ephesians 5.27. Leaven, 13.33, speaks of corruption subtly at work; it is both evil doctrine, 16.6, 12, and wickedness, 1 Corinthians 5.8. If the mustard seed describes the outward growth of the professing church, then the hidden leaven describes its inner corruption. But the Lord has something hidden also, 13.44. Israel is His treasure, and for now it is hidden in the field of the world but precious to Him.

Chapter 14
Food for the Crowd

The voice that once cried out in the wilderness had been violently stopped. When Herod heard of Jesus, his evil conscience concluded that John had returned from the dead and was performing miracles in resurrection; something he never did in life, John 10:41.

Upon hearing of the martyrdom of the Baptist, Jesus sought a place of solitude. However, he would not be granted tranquility. The crowd followed him and rudely interrupted his meditation. It is pleasant to observe the manner in which Jesus received them. There was no irritation, no sign of annoyance. He was moved, not by resentment, but "had compassion on them, and healed their sick," 14:14.

Later, he fed the whole multitude, which numbered more than five thousand, with only five loaves and two fish. We must observe the way in which the Lord worked. First, He required the disciples to bring Him their limited resources; then He wonderfully multiplied this provision; finally, He gave it back to them to distribute to the multitude. Today He still desires to employ His disciples in ministering to the needs of humanity. He asks us to bring to Him what little we have; He blesses it in His own way, and commissions us to distribute it to others. It is an unspeakable privilege to be so used on the Lord's behalf, but at the same time it is our responsibility.

That night the disciples were rowing hard in the troubled waters of the Sea of Galilee when Jesus approached them, walking on those waters. To calm their fears, he said simply, "Take courage! I am he." His words, "It is finished" in John 19:30 direct us to the Cross and a salvation that is complete; his words in Matthew 4:4, "It is written," direct us to his Word and a weapon that enables us to overcome the evil one; and, his words here, ""I am," direct us to his Person and his continuing presence in the midst of all our struggles and anxieties.

15.1 to 31

Great Faith

———

Clearly the woman of Canaan was in great need; her daughter was severely tormented by a demon. But it seemed at first that her request would be denied. In the first instance the Lord was silent at her entreaty, and when He spoke, nothing He said was cause for encouragement. To his disciples, who were interested in the case, he said, "I am not sent," and at the woman's insistence he said, "It is not well." It was not that he lacked compassion for either the woman or the daughter. The impediment was rather in the way she addressed Him at the beginning. She called Him Son of David, a distinctly Jewish title. Others who did so were blessed at once, 9.27, 20.30. But they were Jews and this one was a Gentile. She did not have the facility to approach Him as Son of David; her basis of approach was inappropriate.

The Lord makes him see the outside place that corresponds to him, comparing his position to that of the domestic animal in contrast to the privileges of the sons of the house (who represent the people of Israel). His faith was magnificently imposed in the answer he gave. She did not contradict Him; rather, she turned the Lord's words around to support what she was asking. She took the very subject He had employed, and with the certainty of faith sent it back. Recognizing now her true position, she affirmed that even the little dog in the house could expect a certain portion from her.

She was not trying to deny Israel what was hers, nor was she seeking for herself the share that belonged to "the children". But surely there would be "crumbs" that she could ask for. Her faith in Him was such that she likened to mere crumbs the power necessary for Him to deal with her daughter. Great was her faith and, like Jacob, she struggled and prevailed. "Be it done unto thee as thou wilt," He said. At first it seemed that she would be denied the smallest favor, but now He opens to her His vast treasures and resources, inviting her to take all that she needs. May God give us the faith to "pray without ceasing," 1 Thessalonians 5:17. Let us remember that His delays are not necessarily His refusals!

15.32 to 16.12
Full Consecration

———

This was the second time Jesus had fed a large crowd with just a few loaves and fishes. The baskets that were filled with leftovers on this second occasion were much larger than the baskets in the miracle of chapter 14. Nevertheless, the number of slides involved teaches us a simple but valuable lesson. When the Lord fed more than five thousand with five loaves and two fishes, the twelve small baskets were filled with pieces. Now He uses seven loaves and a few fish to feed a smaller number of people. We might well have expected to find more than twelve baskets full after the event, but it turns out that there were only seven.

Why do the results of this miracle not seem to be as outstanding as in the other case? The explanation is in Mark 8:10, 14, where we are informed that immediately after the incident the disciples are left with "one loaf" in their boat. Jesus had plainly asked them, "How many loaves have you?" It seems that they forgot, or purposely left, one in the boat. The blessing diminished because, being tested, they failed to give and consecrate to Him all that they had. If we are to experience full blessing in the Lord's service,

He must have everything of ours. Does he have it?

Later he warned his disciples to beware of the leaven of the Pharisees and Sadducees, 16:6. He was referring to doctrine but the disciples mistakenly understood him to be referring to the fact that they had not brought food. He reminded them of the two recent occasions when he had fed large crowds. Therefore, it would have been relatively little for Him to feed Himself and the disciples. In the light of previous events, they should never have imagined that the provision of food would be problematic for Jesus.

When new needs confront us, we should consider how the Lord has proven Himself to us in the past, and trust that He will do so again. David provides us with an example of the reasoning of faith when he said, "The Lord, who delivered me out of the paws of the lion and out of the paws of the bear, He will also deliver me out of the hand of this Philistine," 1 Samuel 17:37. Paul reasoned in the same way; 2 Corinthians 1 10: "he delivered us, and delivers us, and in whom we hope he will yet deliver us." What about us?

16.13 to 28

The Sufferings of Christ

―――

It is clear that Jesus' personality left a deep impression on the people of his day. No doubt they discerned qualities in the Lord that led them to identify him with one and the other as in 16.14. He shared with the Baptist a relentless rejection of sin and hypocrisy; he was characterized by the same courage and bravery that men associated with Elijah and at the same time by a compassion akin to that of the prophet of lamentations, Jeremiah.

But Peter knew that those characters and their times had already passed into history. Now no one less than the Christ, the Son of God, was present. Thanks to all that he had heard and seen of the Lord, Peter had been enabled by the Father to penetrate the secret of the Lord's person, 16.16. All in all,

Pedro had a long way to go.

He did not hold the popular idea of Jesus' identity but he definitely did hold the popular concept of what being the Messiah involved. His messianic notion fell far short of the truth of the case; therefore, when Jesus spoke of dying in Jerusalem, Peter objected.

Peter was right about the Lord's titles but wrong about his mission. The cross was a stumbling block to him, and this showed that his ideas of the Messiah had been shaped by men and not by God. In the divine purpose, the sufferings of Christ were an integral part of his mission, 20.28. Later Peter came to understand all this. In his first Epistle he speaks in every chapter of the sufferings, and in every mention he associates them with the title Christ.

In the words that Peter spoke at Caesarea Philippi, Jesus heard two different echoes from the past. He knew the first as the voice of his Father, who had declared at his baptism that he was his divine and only Son, 16.16, 17. He knew also the voice of the devil, who had counseled him in the temptation in the wilderness to lay aside the cross and proceed directly to the throne, 16.22, 23. He had a Church to build, 16.16 18. Such was His love for this Church that Christ was willing to give Himself for it, Ephesians 5.25.

Chapter 17
Jesus Only

B oth at his baptism and on the mountain of transfiguration, God pointed to the Lord Jesus as his beloved Son in whom he was well pleased, 3:17, 17:5. On the mountain he singled him out as above the best of men. In every sense the Lord is greater than Moses or Elijah. Both were prophets who had spoken the word of the Lord, but God was now speaking "by His Son," Heb. 1.1, 2. "Hear ye Him," He said, 17.5.

Both Moses and Elijah were mountain men (Sinai and Carmel) but on this mountain they should not figure but let us see "Jesus alone". Both Moses and Elijah controlled great waters. Moses had to use a rod, Exodus 14:16, and Elijah a blanket, 2 Kings 2:8. When Jesus controlled the waters, his word was enough, 8.26.

The ways in which Moses and Elijah retired from this world were quite unusual. Moses died on a mountain because of a sin he had committed, and God himself buried him. Elijah was translated directly to glory. The way in which the Lord retired was the sum of these two cases. Like Moses, he died on a mountain (but for our sins) and the circumstances of his burial were established by God, Isaiah 53 9. Like Elijah, he was "taken up into heaven," Luke 24.51.

In view of the circumstances that confronted him, there was a time when Moses was determined to resign. He said his responsibility was too much, Numbers 11.14. In 1 Kings 19.4 Elijah also found the path too difficult, and cried, "Enough is enough!" The Lord faced waves of opposition that the other two never knew, but he pressed on until he could announce that "It is finished."

Moses and Elijah could influence only the outward behavior of the people. They were not able to change hearts and, consequently, neither the most outstanding promises of the people, Exodus 19.8 ("All that the LORD has said, we will do"), nor their confessions, 1 Kings 18.39 ("The LORD is God, the LORD is God!"), came to nothing. Jesus inaugurated a new covenant in his blood. One of its conditions is written on our hearts. Peter was rebuked because he put the Lord on the same level with Moses and Elijah, 17.4, 5. He learned his lesson. In recounting the transfiguration, it takes place for "Jesus alone," 2 Peter 1.16 to 18.

18.1 to 14

A Child Like This

When the disciples asked who would be the greatest in the kingdom of heaven, the Lord used a little child as an apt illustration for his answer. A child is ignorant of pride, haughtiness and selfish ambition. The Lord warned the disciples that, by not reversing the course of their thoughts and learning the confidence and humility of a child, they could never begin to understand what it means to be ruled by God. By not abandoning their selfishness, they would not enter the kingdom of God, much less be the greatest in it.

True humility does not consist in thinking bad things about ourselves, but in thinking nothing about ourselves. A disciple needs this kind of humility if he is to achieve greatness in the kingdom of heaven, 18.4. But it is not only that the disciple must be humble and unpretentious about himself, but that he must assume a healthy attitude toward others who believe in Jesus. For such a person to receive one of them is to receive the Lord himself. He is committing the worst of sins that makes the path of the humble brother more difficult. It is better not to live than not to love, 18.6. Any tendency in the disciple that gives rise to temptation or stumbling to another must be dealt with in the most severe manner - whatever the cost to oneself.

The passage emphasizes that humble believers are not, as a rule, held in high esteem in the eyes of the world; they are repeatedly referred to as "little children" and "little ones", 18.3, 5, 6, 10,14. The sin that beset many Pharisees and teachers of the law was disdain for the unlearned and those who in their judgment were unworthy of attention. The disciple, however, must be careful not to despise any of the Lord's "little ones".

The Lord gives three reasons. They are cared for by high and noble beings who enjoy the presence and favor of God, 18:10. They were sought and saved by the Son of Man, for whom they are of inexplicable esteem, 18.11 to 13. And, third, they are the object of the Father's care and grace, 18.14. The "little ones" may be looked down upon by worldlings, but their welfare is of supreme importance to the holy angels, to the divine Shepherd and to the Father, who will not allow one of them to be lost. May the Lord deliver us from trampling on those whom He describes as "the apple of His eye," Zechariah 2:8.

18.15 to 35

Forgiveness

———

Peter interrupted the Lord to ask for clarification of a point. The Lord had been outlining the procedure to be followed in the case of one Christian doing something wrong against another, vv 15 to 17, and had implied that the repentant brother should be forgiven. Okay, but Peter wanted to know what would be the case if that other committed a second offense... or a third? How many times should the Christian forgive another before saying enough is enough? Peter suggested that perhaps seven times would be a reasonable limit.

The Lord answered him with a parable, 18:23-34. The servant of a certain king owed him a fabulous sum of money and begged for a place to pay it off. It turned out that the king granted more than the servant asked for. Instead of setting a time limit for the cancellation of the debt, he forgave it entirely. The servant was free. Shortly thereafter, this same man found another servant who owed him an unimportant sum. The colleague asked for a time limit to cancel the debt, but was refused, and rather he was treated very badly.

When the king heard of the case, he rightly treated the first servant without mercy. However our brothers and sisters may sin against us, their duty to us will always be a small thing in comparison with the number of sins that God in his grace has forgiven us for. The fingers of one hand are usually enough to count the occasions when others have wronged us, but an electronic computer could not keep count of the times we have offended our Lord! Yet, in grace he has forgiven us all.

We need to constantly remind ourselves of the cost and importance of our forgiveness. Not only will it make us love the Lord more, Luke 7:41-43, but it will also make us more willing to forgive those who offend us. No numerical limits can be set to forgiveness in the kingdom of heaven, for the only way to enter it is unrestricted forgiveness. If we always forgive our brother from the heart, 18.35, we won't even know how many times, because we won't keep count! Be careful to keep Ephesians 4.32: "Be kind to one another, tenderhearted, forgiving one another, just as God also in Christ forgave you."

19.1 to 15
Do not impede them

A question asked by the Pharisees gave rise to the Lord's explanation of His doctrine on marriage. He set aside the law, which had been given because of their hardness of heart, Deuteronomy 24:1 to 4. He referred to God's original purpose according to which a man and a woman were joined together and made one in the sight of God.

The Lord therefore re-established the true character of the marriage bond. This union did not admit of rupture except for the exceptional circumstance of fornication. The disciples expressed the opinion that if marriage was so compromising then it would be better never to marry! Some men, the Lord explained, would certainly never marry or participate in the coming into the world of His children. The highest motive in this regard was for those who would renounce family life for the sake of the kingdom of heaven.

It is evident that the apostles understood this in the sense that marriage and family constitute an undesirable second choice for a disciple. It was "then" that children were presented to him. He does not tell us who presented them, 19:13, Mark 10:13, Luke 18:15, but no doubt some parents were involved. In any case, the self-appointed guardians were quick to bar access to the Lord! It seemed obvious to them that He, having thus spoken of marriage, would not be pleased to be disturbed by a group of children with their fathers and mothers.

Therefore, "the disciples rebuked them". They were sure that He would have no interest in children. How wrong they were! Jesus was indignant, Mark 10:14. Calling them children, He rebuked the disciples, Luke

18:16. To avoid any misunderstanding, He expressed His interest in children by a positive and a negative commandment: such should be allowed to come and not forbidden.

Then He not only laid His hands on them, 19.15, but took them in His arms and blessed them, Mark 10.16. We can associate this with the interest He took in the children's play in the marketplaces, 11.16, 17. Indeed, His last message before He was crucified included a reference to children, Luke 23.3 8. Let all those who work among children and youth, whether in Sunday school, youth meetings, day school, or home, be encouraged. The Lord was interested in children.

19.16 to 20.16
My Motive in Service

The Lord told the parable of the hired servants, 20:1 to 15, to illustrate and explain his saying: "The first shall be last, and the last first". The message of the parable is in the way the day's wages are distributed at the end of the day. Those who worked the least amount of time were paid first. When it was the turn of those who worked twice as long, they received the same pay, and they did not like it. The men who started first were placed last, and to make matters worse they were paid less in proportion to the work they did. But they had agreed beforehand as to their day's wages, 20.2, and everything was done in orderly fashion.

They had wanted to know what they were going to receive for their efforts. In contrast, the workers who joined last did not insist on negotiating a rate beforehand; they were willing to trust the honesty and generosity of the vineyard owner. This second attitude paid high dividends! He was fair to the former, and generous to the latter. The negotiators, "the first", found themselves in the last position in line to receive the reward.

The parable was for the benefit of the disciples, who had listened when the Lord demanded that the rich young ruler leave everything to follow Jesus. The promise was that he would have "treasure in heaven," 19:21. The young man was not willing to pay the price, but they had paid it. Having met the Lord's conditions, they wanted to know more details about the "treasure" they considered theirs to receive, 19.27. The Lord graciously promised them positions of authority in his kingdom and a hundredfold reward for all the earthly ties they had sacrificed.

Then he told them the parable. In effect he warned them not to occupy themselves unduly with the details of their reward. A little done here in the spirit of love and devotion was worth more than much done in the spirit of a hireling. The heavenly reward is promised to us as an encouragement in our service for Christ, but it should not be the motive for such service. "The love of Christ constraineth us," 2 Corinthians 5:14. Most assuredly we can trust the Lord to reward justly. He is not unjust to forget, Hebrews 6.10.

20.17 to 34

True Greatness

Like so many others, Salome hoped that the Lord would redeem Israel from the hated oppression of Rome to establish an earthly, political kingdom. She coveted a place of prominence and power for her children in that kingdom, and they harbored the same longing. Jesus questioned her ability to partake of her cup and her baptism. He referred to the suffering that lay ahead of her, but they misunderstood him altogether.

In the Old Testament drinking from a cup could be understood for good or evil, and James and John interpreted his words as a reference to blessings in the kingdom. Therefore, they affirmed that they could indeed participate in his kingdom. With sadness Jesus confirmed that the two of them would experience "the sharing of his sufferings," Philippians 3:10. The position of eminence, however, was not theirs to give. The other apostles were upset because of this selfish request, and deeply resented the attempt to secure chief positions.

Yet the resentment of the ten men was rooted in precisely the same soil as the solicitude of the two. Clearly all the twelve regarded the kingdom of Christ as similar to the Roman empire with its procurators, kings and emperors. This eagerness for self-good on the part of the two brothers, and the dislike of the other disciples, proceeded from the same worldly concept of greatness. The man in authority is considered to be the greatest. They were totally wrong! The rules of Jesus' kingdom went in the opposite direction. The greatest of all was the servant of all. James and John should not have sought a position where they would be served, and the others should not have been so upset at the prospect of serving them.

The Lord cited His own example in life and death. He had come to serve and to give his life for others. His words find appropriate commentary today in the reading. His willingness to serve is seen in 20:29 to 34. Others thought the blind unworthy of His attention, but He stopped and gave them sight. "What would ye have me do unto you?" are the words of one who serves. His willingness to lay down His life is explicitly stated in 20:17 to 19. We have to face the question: would I rather be a servant or a ruler among God's people?

21.1 to 16

The King Comes

The Lord's entry into Jerusalem was accompanied by much enthusiasm and excitement. May God allow us to experience a little of the pleasant sensation that always comes from seeing the King in His beauty, Isaiah 33:17. We should observe four qualities of this King.

Poverty: The Lord had a genuine "need", 21.3. He rode on a borrowed donkey for the obvious reason that he had no beast of his own. We are not surprised. He preached from someone else's boat, illustrated his message using someone else's coin, took the Passover in someone else's chamber, and, after death, would be laid in someone else's tomb. The cloaks of his disciples would be his couch. He who rode on another's donkey was able to create a chariot of diamonds and gold. Indeed, he who was rich became poor!

Tenderness: The prophet had predicted that Christ would employ two animals. Jesus rode on the smaller of the two, John 12:14, but demanded that they bring the larger one as well. Perhaps the donkey and her foal had never been separated and He was interested in how each would react. Few men would have accommodated the detail, but such consideration for others was characteristic of the one who drew water from the rock to water the beasts, Numbers 20:11, and who had pity on Nineveh because of its many animals, Jonah 4:1.

Humility: The King was entering his royal city. He possessed the authority of king, an authority recognized not only by men, but by beasts, 21.6, 7. As to this, it is significant that the animal had never been tamed, Luke 19.30. Nevertheless, the King's conduct was characterized by a total absence of any ostentation or ceremony. For the Lord, greatness went hand in hand with meekness.

Courage: He did not walk with a glittering sword in his hand; there was no helmet on his forehead, nor a fierce horse making capers. He rode on a colt, as did ancient monarchs who went out on missions of peace. Yet his face was that of a warrior. He had come to the holy city to fight for a kingdom, though not a kingdom of this world. In five days he must die. A cross would be the chariot of triumph from which he would crush our many enemies. Knowing full well what the battle ahead would be like, John 18:4, the Lion of Judah turned back for nothing, Proverbs 30:30.

21.17 to 22.14
Sheets Only

J esus and His disciples left Bethany early one morning, and in the cool
spring air He felt hungry. A solitary fig tree was growing out of the
rocky ground beside the road. It was not the season for figs, but the bush,
covered with leaves, caught His attention. It is well known that the fruit
develops first on a fig tree, and then the leaves.

Out of season, this bush had sprouted leaves early, suggesting that there
would be figs underneath. The Lord, however, found "leaves only," 21.19.
The foliage lied; there was no fruit! Jesus pronounced a command and
at once the bush began to dry up. The disciples did not notice anything
unusual. It was the next morning that they observed the effect of the
Lord's words, Mark 11 20.

The fig tree had been used as a symbol of the nation of Israel, Joel 1:7.

The Lord therefore chose the premature and barren germination of this
fig tree as an emblem of a people who, with all their great profession
and formal ritual, were destitute of the fruits of righteousness, without
which mere outward forms were worse than useless. The fig leaves of
Israel constituted an effort to cover their true nakedness before God, just
as fig leaves had been used to cover the nakedness of man and woman in
the Garden of Eden, Gen. 3.7. The bush, then, must be destroyed.

We at one time had only leaves, but it is exciting to remember that God
has revealed Jesus to us only, 17.8. He demanded to believe only, Luke
8.50. But are we only talking, or is the fruit of the Spirit really being
produced in our lives? Galatians 5.22, 23. Then the Lord spoke of the
failures of his people who considered themselves righteous, and of their

leaders in particular, 21.45. In the parable of the two sons, 21:28-32, he contrasted between them with their loud profession of obedience and the multitude of rejecters who repented and found salvation under John's ministry.

In the parable of the vineyard, 11:33-46, He spoke of His responsibility and His failure to fulfill it. In the parable of the wedding feast, 22:1 to 14, He described their privileges in the gospel. They were the guests who refused to attend. Let us take care that our profession is real, that we fulfill our responsibilities and be thankful for our privileges.

22.15 to 46

Whose image?

———

Several Herodians and disciples of the Pharisees challenged the Lord. The question they threw at him, however, was not his own, but the inspiration of the religious leaders of the nation the Pharisees, 22.15, with the chief priests and scribes, Luke 20.19, 20. The question they had selected was one over which the nation was divided. They arranged for representatives of both sides to be present. The Herodians represented the party loyal to the Roman government, while the Pharisees were strongly opposed to it and had great sympathy for the many rebellions against the emperor. The purpose was to set a trap for Jesus and to entangle him in their words. Since A.D. 6 Palestine had been governed by the Romans through procurators. The payment of tribute was one of the most tangible and hated symbols of that government.

The Jewish delegation came with sweet words of flattery, 22:16, and with the intent to disarm any suspicions Jesus had. He perceived everything! They intended to leave the Lord in a great dilemma, and it would have been fatal to assume one position or the other. To say yes would have been to acknowledge Caesar's royal authority and to renounce any claim by Jesus to be the Messiah. The Pharisees were more than willing to accuse him before the people as an enemy of their nationalistic aspirations. The rulers expected, however, that he would say no. In this case the Herodians were prepared to accuse him before Pilate as an enemy of the Roman state, Luke 20.20, 23.2. Their plans had been cunningly formulated and skillfully executed!

The Lord answered them with perfect wisdom, as He would do when questioned later, 22.23 to 40. He pointed them to the image, name, and titles bearing his own coinage, which gave ample evidence of Roman dominion. The Lord asserted that to pay tax to Caesar was simply to return to him his own. But he went beyond this. Man bears an image also, though marred and worn, 22.21, Gen. 1.26, 27. Jesus reminded those lords of God's rights over them. They left Him; their purpose had been frustrated. We too must render "to Caesar" what is his and to God the things that are His, Romans 13.1 to 7, 12.1, 2.

Chapter 23
Blessed is He

The last verses give us the last words that the Lord Jesus addressed to his nation. It is very touching to see His compassion for Israel revealed, now that He considers His ministry among His people. How sad it is that He had to speak also of His deliberate rejection of those who chose not to be saved. A hen and her chicks provide Him with an exquisite picture of the protection and care He had offered, 23.37. But of what dreadful resistance the human will was capable!

Israel would not. How much happier are those of whom it can be said, "He shall cover thee with his feathers, and under his wings shalt thou be safe," Psalm 91:4. Jesus had spoken of a gnat and a camel, to highlight the incongruous actions of a people who concentrated on the relevantly trivial matters at the expense of the important of the spiritual life.

He had also mentioned serpents and vipers, as a description of the ungodly character of those who were like their father the devil, John 8:44 with Rev. 12:9. The nation no longer saw Him as a merciful Savior offering redemption; but one day they would recognize Him as their Deliverer and receive Him as such, Then the acclamation of the multitude would be heard again! 23.39.

The Lord's mournful lamentation immediately followed a devastating denunciation. The works of those who abhorred the truth and rejected God were done only to gain the applause of men. The woes which Jesus pronounced against them furnish us with a full-length portrait of the hypocrite in all his false profession and shameful inconsistency.

There were eight woes for all*, and we are taken through the eight woes uttered by Isaiah the prophet against his contemporaries**.

* 23.14,15,16,23,25,27,29, ** Isaiah 3.9,11, 5.8,11,18,20,21,22.

There was, however, an important difference between Isaiah and Jesus. Confronted with the majesty and holiness of Jehovah of hosts, the prophet was obliged to utter one more "woe" - against himself! But not so the Lord! He closed his speech, not with a lamentation but with a benediction: "Blessed is he who comes in the name of the Lord". Isaiah added, "Woe is me!" Jesus, considering Himself, added, "Blessed is He."

Chapter 24
The Coming of the Son of Man

The pages of world history are turning fast and are often covered with blood. Our civilization is permeated by barbarity and savagery; in many places the foundations of human government and society are shaking; the human capacity to destroy is appalling. No wonder, then, that people exclaim with God's prophet, "My Lord, what shall be the end of these things?" Daniel 12.8. The description the Lord gave of the end of the age provides part of the answer.

The disciples had asked two questions. First: "When will these things be?" referring to the fall of Jerusalem and the destruction of the temple of which He had spoken at that time. Those events were to take place some forty years later. Second: "What sign shall there be of thy coming, and of the end of the age?" (That is, of the age). This is a double event that has not yet taken place. Therefore, his answer covered events that will take place over many centuries.

He answered the first question with a description of the general signs of the present age, 24:4 to 14, and the second with a mention of the special signs at the end of the age, 24:15 to 51. We must clearly distinguish between the characteristics of the entire age and those preceding His return to reign. The "wars and rumors of war" are not indications of the Lord's return. Of such things the Lord specifically said, "but the end is not yet." The signs that warn of His coming to reign as the Son of Man are "the abomination of desolation" and "great tribulation".

Even though the passage refers to Israel in the first instance, there are several practical applications for us. Great emphasis is placed on human ignorance as to when the Son of Man will return, 24.36, 42,44, 25.13. We do not learn here when the rapture will be. Therefore, we must keep a condition of constant expectation lest we find ourselves unprepared, 25.43.

The conviction that the Lord may come at any moment affects one's attitude toward others, 24:45-51. The wicked servant suspected that his master had delayed his return. When Israel doubted that Moses would return, they also began to misbehave, Exodus 32:1 to 6. If we do not live in the light of the Lord's return, we are liable to want to turn away from Him in shame when He returns, 1 John 2:28.

25.1 to 30
Opportunities Seized

The parable of the virgins teaches us to be expectant and prepared for the coming of the Lord. The parable of the talents teaches us the importance of serving him well while we await his coming.

The "talents" (silver coins) represent the opportunities to be useful and render the service that the Lord assigns us. They do not represent our ability or capacity. They are a figure of the scope He provides us to serve Him, which, by the way, is fixed according to our ability, 25.15. He neither demands nor expects us to do more than we can.

Within their limited spheres, the first two servants acted with drive and righteousness. Their master praised them and decided to make greater use of them, assigning them positions of greater trust and responsibility.

The third servant had no profit to offer the master. He claimed that he had done nothing with his coin because he did not want to disturb his master, but the master exposed the falsity and inadequacy of this mere excuse. The truth was that the man had fled from the effort involved in the employment of his talent. He was "wicked and negligent." The idle coin was taken from the idle servant and given to him who had served well.

The proper and energetic use of our opportunities and possibilities in this world will earn us a reward that will consist partially of greater and permanent opportunities to serve our Lord in His glorious kingdom. The full and faithful employment of our present ability will guarantee us greater and wider opportunities to please Him in the future. Our reward for a job well done will be labors on a scale beyond our imagining, in that day when "His servants shall serve Him, and shall see His face, and His name shall be on their foreheads," Rev. 22:3, 4.

On the other hand, untapped opportunities and undeveloped capabilities will be lost and nullified forever. The divine law is that what a servant gives up through carelessness and imprudence passes on to another. The individual will suffer loss, but the work of God will not. The throne of Saul passes to David and the office of Judas to Matthias. The industrious worker can assume the heavenly service that the idle one is renouncing. Our place in the kingdom will not be assigned in an arbitrary manner but according to the value of which it now proves us.

25.31 to 46
About...

The Lord ended His discourse on the Mount of Olives with a description of the day of examination and review. There is little doubt that the passage contemplates the judgment of the Gentiles by the Messiah with respect to their attitude toward the Jews in the period of the great tribulation, Joel 3:1 to 8.

However, we must be careful not to use its successful dispensational application as a reason to evade the force of its application as an examination of our own consciences. The principle enunciated in verses 40 and 45 still applies to the Lord's people today; indeed, it applies to "the least" among them! The Lord considers everything we do on behalf of His "brethren" to be done on His behalf. This truth underlies His challenge issued to Saul of Tarsus, "Why do you persecute Me?" Acts 26.14.

We can take comfort in the fact that the Lord Jesus knows who among His people are hungry, thirsty, naked, etc. He takes into account all the circumstances of the daily life of all the saints, and can say, "I know... your affliction, and your poverty", Revelation 2.3.

Christ's blessing is reserved for those who have compassion, are kind, and care for the needs of others. Their services are not rendered for reward or because they know that the Lord will count their deeds as done on their behalf. They are rather surprised by such deeds, 25:37-39.

The Lord Jesus proceeds to roundly condemn the sin of neglect, 25:41 to 46. Here it is not those who fail to prepare themselves, as in 25:1 to 13, nor those who resolutely fail to use their opportunities of service for

Him, as in 25:14 to 30, but those who ignore the need of others. It is the sin of doing nothing.

He does not accuse those at his left hand of stealing the food of the poor, but of not feeding them. He does not accuse them of poisoning others, but of not giving them to drink. He does not accuse them of taking clothes from the body of another, but of not clothing the naked. He does not accuse them of injuring the brethren of the Lord himself, but of not visiting them when they are sick. He does not accuse them of persecuting their fellow men, but of not visiting them when they are prisoners.

"To him that knoweth to do good, and doeth it not, to him it is sin," James 4.17.

26.1 to 35
The Anointing at Bethany

J esus was anointed in the house of a leper. It was fitting that the one who was about to be rejected by his nation and rulers should be received into the house of a man who knew something in his own flesh of being "despised and rejected among men."

Mary willingly and profusely poured out on the Lord the precious ointment worth about three hundred denarii, John 12.3, 5. It was a costly gift; a similar jar of ointment was once presented as a gift from the emperor of Persia to the king of Ethiopia! Mary faced a storm of criticism from the disciples, led by Judas; compare 26.8 with John 12.4, 5. Judas pretended to be looking out for the good of the poor but was actually upset because he was not given the opportunity to appropriate funds for his own purposes, John 12.6.

His concept of the value of Jesus was very different from Mary's. She gladly gave the Lord what she had. She gladly gave the Lord what she had, but for Judas this was a waste, for he valued the Lord at nothing more than the price of a slave, that is, thirty pieces of silver. Judas was interested in what he could get for Jesus but Mary was occupied with what he could give her to Jesus.

But even the alabaster of perfume she gave in sacrifice was as nothing in comparison to what He would give for her, 26:26-28. His body and blood would be poured out as well. What significance this must have for us! Mary poured the ointment on the Lord's body in preparation for His burial. It is striking that she was apparently not among the women who went days later to embalm his body, Luke 24:10.

Mary anointed their head, Matt. 26:7, and their feet, John 12:3. Isaiah described the nation of Israel as corrupt "from the sole of the foot to the head," 1.6. In Nebuchadnezzar's dream, the figure of the world empire included a head of fine gold and feet of iron and clay, Daniel 2.31 to 33. But if Judah was sick from head to foot, and if the poor Gentile was decaying from head to foot, things are very different with our "beloved", Song of Solomon 5.10 to 16. In the Lord Jesus Christ there is no corruption or decay, but is "altogether lovely".

Unspoken Prayer

———

Pedro was a better fisherman than spearman. When he lunged at Malco with his spear, he managed to remove only an ear and not a head.

The Lord rebuked his faithful but erring disciple. He first enunciated the broad principle that those who live by the sword will die by the sword, 26.52. Then He explained to Peter a prayer that He had been able to pray. If the Lord had prayed thus, He would not have suffered the agony just now in the theft; He would not have had to drink the cup of such bitterness; He would have escaped ignominy, insults and vulgar violence before Caiaphas.

What could the Lord have asked for? Angels! The Savior was in the garden of Gethsemane, in the area described by the prophet Joel as the valley of Jehoshaphat, about which he says: "Cause thy mighty ones to come thither, O Lord," Joel 3:9 to 13. Possibly Michael and his angels, Rev. 12.7, were on their feet at that very moment to sweep Judas and his "many people" into eternity. But it would not be so.

What could the Lord have asked for? Legions! Not only were the temple guard and the servants of the chief priests and scribes nearby, but there stood before Jesus a Roman captain and his company, John 18:12. The Lord was telling Peter that He could command a support that would far exceed any number of forces that His enemies could muster.

And how many legions? Twelve. Eleven of his disciples accompany him as well. Each of them could count on a whole legion of angelic hosts! In a single night, a single angel destroyed 185,000 Syrians, 2 Kings 19:35.

On this basis, twelve legions, or 72,000, could wipe out a population three and a half times that of the world today. Such a display of force was at Christ's disposal if He only asked for it in prayer, but He would never avail Himself of it. His hour had come. God's will must be done, Matthew 26:42. The Scriptures must be fulfilled.

27.1 to 32

In Place of Barabbas

———

Peter stated that the men of Israel denied the Holy One and the Righteous One, and asked to give them a murderer, that they killed the Author of Life; Acts 3.14, 15. He was saying that they gave life to the One who took life, and took life from the One who gave life. However, the irony of the situation went beyond this.

The Jewish council had condemned Jesus as a blasphemer; 26:65, 66. Knowing that such an accusation would be of no importance to Pilate, they prepared political accusations. Pilate could not ignore the charge that Jesus claimed to be "Christ, a king," Luke 23:2. The leaders of Israel falsely imputed to Jesus the political expectations about the Messiah that they themselves harbored.

The Lord had scrupulously avoided giving any support to an uprising against Rome, John 6.15, but now the charge of being precisely the kind of Messiah he had refused to be weighed against him, 4.1 to 10, 16.21 to 23. It was incredible to Pilate that this poor, bound Galilean preacher could have pretended to be a king, and so he examines him as to the nature of his kingship, 27.3, John 18.33 to 38.

Satisfied as to Jesus' innocence and confident as to the outcome of the trial, Pilate offers to release to the people either Jesus or Barabbas. The people choose Barabbas, largely due to the subtle influence of the chief priests and elders. A patriotic adventurer, who recognized no messiah but the one with the sword, proved more attractive to the people and their leaders than the Man who had just suffered without resistance; 1 Peter 2:23.

The rulers had professed that He was a threat to Rome, but they abandoned Him because they knew He was not. They said they wanted to crucify Him because He said that His kingdom was not of this world, but they were pleased to see Him die because they knew that He truly was not.

The culminating anger was in the fact that the governor was forced to release a man guilty of precisely the same kind of crime that the leaders had tried to assign to Jesus. The Lord was taken out to be crucified instead of one who represented the kind of messianic hope He resolutely refused to offer.

Barabbas must have known that Jesus died in his place. We also know that he gave himself for us; Ephesians 5:2.

27.33 to 66

The Death of Christ Had Four Immediate Effects

First, his death served to open a way to the holiest place in the temple. The torn veil demonstrated that the sacrifice Jesus had offered was sufficient to "bring us to God," 1 Peter 3:18. The unbroken veil, along with many other details of the Jewish system, had indicated that "the way into the Most Holy Place had not yet been made manifest," Hebrews 9:3 to 8. Before the cross of Christ, entering that place resulted in death, Leviticus 16.2; but from the cross onward death is for the one who remains outside! When God parted the heavens, 3.16, 17, it was to declare His pleasure in the person of His Son; when He parted the veil, it was to declare His pleasure in the work of His Son.

Second, his death served to open the tombs of the saints. Although the tombs were opened at this time, it is clear that their bodies were resurrected and came out of the tombs only when the Lord had already risen. Then Jesus manifested himself personally, "not to all the people, but to the witnesses whom God had ordained beforehand," Acts 10:41. The presence in Jerusalem of resurrected believers constituted a testimony of his resurrection before those who had rejected him.

Third, his death and the circumstances of his death served to open the heart of the Roman centurion. Perhaps he had heard when the Jews declared to Pilate that Jesus claimed to be the Son of God, John 19.7. No doubt he came to believe that he was, although the Jews refused to accept that truth, 27.40, 43,54. For Paul, it was the resurrection that declared to him that Jesus was the Son of God, Romans 1.4; for the centurion, his death gave the proof.

Fourth, his death gave rise to an open confession on the part of Joseph of Arimathea. That rich man was already a secret disciple, John 19:38, but the cross gave courage to a cowardly spirit. The Lord rested in Joseph's tomb on the seventh day of the week. Previously, he had rested by consummating his creation of the world, Genesis 2.1 to 3, but now he rests because he has consummated his work of redemption, John 19.30.

In creating Adam, the Lord gave him life, Genesis 2.1 to 7, but in redeeming man, he gave his own life, 20.28.

Chapter 28
The Great Commission

———

The stone was taken away to reveal to mankind what the angels already knew: that Jesus had as much power to take back His own life as He had to lay it down, John 10:18. The angel sat on the stone. Note the contrast between the many precautions men took regarding the door of the tomb and the ease with which they were overruled. Thus the courage of Caesar, his guard and his seal! When the angel intervened the guards trembled as did the earth.

The angel addressed the women of the "place where the Lord was laid", 28.6. For us, that place holds the memory of His triumph over death; the tomb remained, but empty. Matthew has made mention of other scenes. In 26.36 there is "a place called Gethsemane," where Jesus agonized in anticipation of the cross. "A place called Golgotha," 27.33, reminds us of his suffering for sin. Angelic appeals led to similar initiatives by Roman soldiers and by women.

The astounding events were reported to the chief priests by some of the guard, and to the disciples by the mouths of the women. Unfortunately, the announcement by the guard was received with greater credulity than that of the ladies, Luke 24.11.

This Gospel ends with the Great Commission, so called, 28:18 to 20. In it we read of an infinite resource: "all power". Satan had claimed that "all this power ... is given unto me", Luke 4.6, but the Lord rightly acknowledges it as His own. He had said that all things were given to Him by His Father, Matt. 11.27 to 29, and therefore He invited all to come to Him. Here He says that all things are His, and He invites men to go for Him. Whoever is to serve Christ effectively must "come and see" before "going and saying".

Luke also speaks of a universal mission: "all nations". The disciples' parish was not restricted now to Israel, as in 10:5, 6; it is the whole world. They confronted all people with the challenge of discipleship and baptism.

We read of unconditional obedience: "all things". We are not free to choose which commandments we will obey: "I esteemed all thy commandments above all things to be right", Psalm 119.128. The New Testament does not allow for a Christianity of one's own liking.

We also read of a continuous presence: "every day". Jesus gives his word: I, who have the power, am always with you who have the task. Enough.

Don't miss out!

Visit the website below and you can sign up to receive emails whenever Bible Sermons publishes a new book. There's no charge and no obligation.

https://books2read.com/r/B-A-MZBS-MVAGC

BOOKS2READ

Connecting independent readers to independent writers.

Did you love *Analyzing Notes in the Book of Matthew: Fulfillments of Old Testament Prophecies*? Then you should read *Analyzing Labor Education in Pentateuch*[1] by Bible Sermons!

[2]

This book builds on Understanding Work through the Pentateuch by delving into biblical verses and principles for a Christian perspective on work relationships today. We explore how God designed our work, for what purpose we created it, and how we can understand this to live effectively both inside and outside the workplace. Using the Pentateuch as a starting point, we will examine topics such as the meaning, control and direction of work, work ethics, justice, and resources. These truths will help us formulate a greater understanding of our vocations and contribute to the world around us. *With this book you will learn to see*

---

1. https://books2read.com/u/3R0XXD

2. https://books2read.com/u/3R0XXD

your work from a Christian perspective - that there is nothing wrong with work but that it is a blessing and privilege.

Also by Bible Sermons

Notes in the New Testament

Analyzing Notes in the Book of Matthew: Fulfillments of Old Testament Prophecies

Analyzing Notes in the Book of Mark: Finding Peace in Difficult Times

Overflying The Bible

Bible Introduction: Overflying The Bible from Genesis by Brethren in the Faith

Chronological Prophecy: Things That Will Happen on Earth

Bible Study: Genesis 1. Creation in Six Days

The Education of Labor in the Bible

Analyzing the Teaching of Labor in Exodus: From Slavery to Liberation

Analyzing the Labor Education in Leviticus: The Spirit of the Law at Work

Analyzing the Labor Education in Numbers: Israel's Desert Experience for Today's Challenges

Analyzing the Labor Education in Deuteronomy: A Perspective on Working Life Today

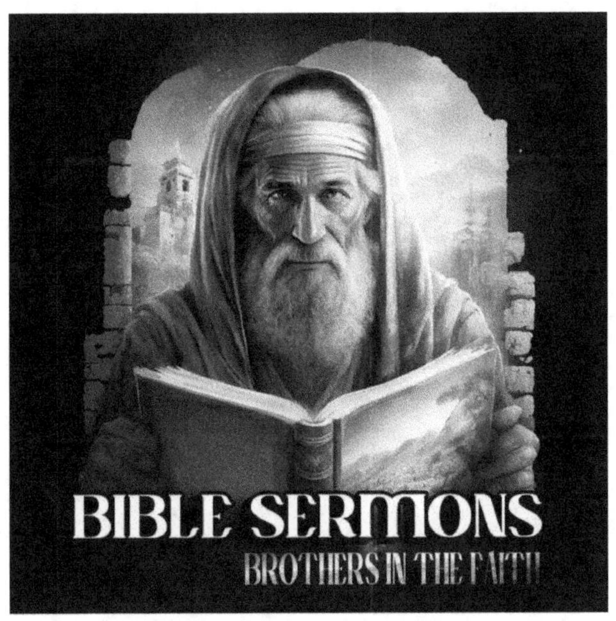

About the Author

This bible study series is perfect for Christians of any level, from children to youth to adults. It provides an engaging and interactive way to learn the Bible, with activities and discussion topics that will help deepen your understanding of scripture and strengthen your faith. Whether you're a beginner or an experienced Christian, this series will help you grow in your knowledge of the Bible and strengthen your relationship with God. Led by brothers with exemplary testimonies and extensive knowledge of scripture, who congregate in the name of the Lord Jesus Christ throughout the world.

www.ingramcontent.com/pod-product-compliance
Lightning Source LLC
Chambersburg PA
CBHW071350130726
47996CB00002B/873